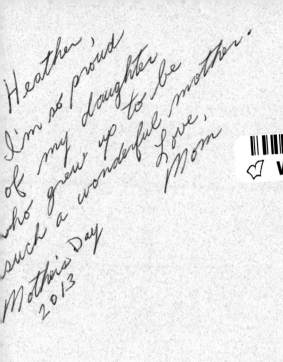

Heather,
I'm so proud
of my daughter
who grew up to be
such a wonderful mother.
Love,
Mom

Mother's Day
2013

a special gift
for my daughter

_____

_____

_____

With Love,

_____

_____

date

Stories, sayings, and scriptures to Encourage and Inspire the...

hugs™

for
Daughters

CHRYS HOWARD

Personalized Scriptures by
LEANN WEISS

HOWARD
PUBLISHING CO.

Our purpose at Howard Publishing is to:

- *Increase faith* in the hearts of growing Christians
- *Inspire holiness* in the lives of believers
- *Instill hope* in the hearts of struggling people everywhere

Because He's coming again!

Hugs for Daughters © 2001 by Chrys Howard
All rights reserved. Printed in the United States of America

Published by Howard Publishing Co., Inc.,
3117 North 7th Street, West Monroe, LA 71291-2227

01 02 03 04 05 06 07 08 09 10   10 9 8 7 6 5 4 3 2 1

Paraphrased Scriptures © 2001 LeAnn Weiss, 3006 Brandywine Dr.,
Orlando, FL 32806; 407-898-4410

Edited by Philis Boultinghouse
Interior design by LinDee Loveland

Library of Congress Cataloging-in-Publication Data

Howard, Chrys, 1953–
    Hugs for daughters : stories, sayings, and scriptures to encourage and inspire the— /
Chrys Howard ; personalized scriptures by LeAnn Weiss.
    p. cm.
    ISBN 1-58229-214-0
    1. Parents—Prayer-books and devotions—English. 2. Daughters—Religious life. I.
Weiss, LeAnn. II. Title.

    BV4529 .H695 2001
    242'.643—dc21

                                                            2001039589

Scripture quotations taken from the Holy Bible, New International Version, © 1973, 1978,
1984 International Bible Society. Used by permission of Zondervan Bible Publishers.

I dedicate this book to *my precious daughters—*
Korie, who was born on October 24, 1973,
with a gentle spirit and tender heart, and
Ashley, who was born on March 1, 1978,
with a twinkle in her eye and a spring in her step.

Thank you, *God,*
for blessing me with daughters
who have been more than children—
they have been and
continue to be my *best friends.*

contents

a daughter

Where did she get those bright, blue eyes
And the dimple in her chin?
Where did the natural curl come from
And the fairness of her skin?

They came from me, I proudly say.
Yes, we're really much the same.
Sometimes I think we're just alike;
We just have different names.

But, wait a minute, whose laugh is that?
And my hair is blond, not brown.
And I don't like to run and fish
Or dig worms from the ground.

Those traits came from her dad, you see,
Along with a tender heart,
So I guess it's only fair to say
He also played a part.

Neither of us can understand
Why her nose turns up, not down
Or how she can sing harmony
And she never seems to frown.

I guess she's not "just like Mom"—
I know it's for the best—
Because she's also a child of God,
And He created the rest.

chapter one

A
daughter's
delight

My Treasured Daughter,

I am with you and mighty to save.
I take great *delight* in you,
    quieting you with My love
and *rejoicing* over you.

When you *delight* in Me,
I'll give you the things your heart
    truly longs for. My precepts are right,
giving joy to your *heart;* and

My commands are *radiant*,

enlightening your eyes.

Watch Me satisfy your *desires*

with good things.

Love,
Your God of Refuge

—from Zephaniah 3:17; Psalms 37:4; 19:8; 103:5

Daughter, you are so loved! From the first announcement of your coming until today, your mother and father have been "in love" with you. Whether the news that you were a girl was revealed through the video of a sonogram or the mouth of the doctor who helped you into the world, the very words "It's a girl!" conjure up pink dresses, hair bows, and baby dolls. Mommas think of matching dresses; daddies think of tender kisses.

Practically obsolete is the scene of the pacing father waiting down the hall as the delivery of the new baby takes place behind closed doors. Gone are the days of the doctor coming into the "new fathers'" waiting room to announce the arrival of the latest bundle. No, today's modern technology gives new parents months to prepare for the baby girl or boy. Baby rooms are carefully designed, and closets are stuffed full of tiny clothes weeks in advance of the birth. It's even common practice to call babies by name while they're still in the womb. All because you are deeply loved.

You've probably heard it said that when Jesus was asked how much He loved us, He stretched out His arms and was nailed to a cross. In other words, He loves us—and you—so much that He gave His life for you. And guess what? Your parents would do the same. What an incredible thought!

The best and most beautiful things in the world cannot be seen or even touched. They must be felt with the *heart*.

helen
keller

Sondra had admired the doll in

the store window for weeks,

never asking for it,

only commenting on its beauty.

babe

She looked like a homecoming queen or maybe a rodeo princess. She had a definite "movie star" quality about her. She'd been blessed with long, thick auburn hair and blue eyes the color of a clear Texas sky. And she loved to sing and play music. The fiddle, the banjo, and the piano were like obedient servants to her masterful touch. Her nickname was "Babe" for no other reason than that she was the baby girl of her family. Babe would have been ninety-four this year had she survived the tragedy. Her sisters were now ninety-eight and ninety-six, so you see, Babe would most likely still be alive.

a daughter's delight

Babe's good looks were far surpassed by her generous heart. The words *kind*, *gentle*, and *tender* were often used to describe her but were not quite adequate. Perhaps adding *patient*, *loving*, and *courteous* would make the description more complete. But again, not totally. There are no words to describe someone who gave her life for someone else. There isn't an adjective powerful enough to express that depth of love. Jesus gave His life for all mankind, and He is honored with words like *Savior*, *Mighty Counselor*, and *Prince of Peace*. Babe gave her life, too, but for just one person—her daughter.

On October 18, 1952, Babe; her husband, Cliff; and their nine-year-old daughter, Sondra, had gotten up early in the morning for the three-hour drive to visit another daughter, Jean. Even though it was October, the Texas air would be hot by midmorning, and air-conditioned cars belonged only to the wealthy; so Cliff had insisted they get an early start. Babe loved the drive to the dairy farm her daughter and son-in-law managed. She relished the Texas countryside where horses and cows and wildflowers provided the perfect backdrop for a Texas sunrise. She delighted in the smell of the fresh-cut grass that filled the car on that fall morning. But most of all, she loved the conversation with her husband and their daughter Sondra.

Sondra had come along "later in life," as some would say. Babe was thirty-six when Sondra was born, but Babe felt young and loved being a mother so much that she never questioned the timing of her pregnancy or her ability to rear another child. Actually, she had begged Cliff to let her have another baby. After getting three other children almost reared, Cliff needed a little convincing. But Babe persevered, and on June 17, 1943, Sondra entered the world. From that moment on, she became Babe's number-one project. She taught Sondra to sing harmony to her lead on her favorite gospel songs and how to stand really still so she could catch a fish for supper. She taught her the value of a clean house and the art of cooking on a budget. No mother cherished a daughter more than Babe did Sondra. By all accounts Babe dressed Sondra like a baby doll and treated her like a doll as well. They were inseparable.

"We'll be there before the cows are milked, won't we?" Babe asked Cliff.

"Pretty sure," he replied. Cliff was man of few words but of many talents. Babe thought he could do anything. He could build a house, fix a car, teach a Sunday school class, and entertain his grandkids with equal ability. Since Sondra had been born, they had had two grandchildren. Babe loved being a grandmother as much as she loved being a mother. This trip today to the dairy farm was to be a survey trip to see if they might want to move there next summer to be closer to the grandkids. Babe was always saying she wanted her ducks in a row, which meant she wanted all her children where she could keep an eye on them. Besides that, they had spent too many years in naval housing. Babe needed a move to the country.

Cliff knew he could find work anywhere, so the thought of moving didn't bother him at all. He just liked to see Babe happy. Babe was only seventeen when he had married her. He had been twenty-seven. He never regretted his decision to marry the beauty from West Texas. He had honored her, cared for her, respected her, and loved her for the past twenty-eight years.

Sondra played in the backseat for most of the trip. Babe had surprised her with a new baby doll for the journey. Sondra had admired the doll in the store window for weeks, never asking for it, only commenting on its beauty. But

Babe loved baby dolls as much as Sondra did and waited for a special occasion to buy it for her daughter. That occasion was a trip out of town. Babe knew the doll would keep Sondra busy. It had done just that for nearly two hours when Babe decided that Sondra needed a change of scenery.

"Sondra, how about riding in the front seat for a while? It's a beautiful day." It was always a treat for Sondra to ride in the front seat between her parents. There was something very comforting and secure about that spot.

"Sure!" Sondra shouted with delight as she jumped over the seat with doll in hand. There were no seat belts in the cars at that time and no air bags. Mothers and fathers didn't think twice about having children sit beside them. Parents were quite used to throwing their arms across the seat to secure a child when the car came to a stop sign or a red light. Sondra snuggled up to her mother and began showing her the bow in her doll's hair.

What happened in the next few minutes would change the course of history for Sondra and Cliff. Out of nowhere, an automobile headed straight toward them. Cliff tried to get out of its path, but the drunk driver in the other vehicle was out of control, and within seconds the two cars collided.

Cliff was pinned under the steering wheel with broken ribs, a crushed hip, and shattered legs. His door was jammed shut, and he couldn't get out. Babe had locked her door at the beginning of the trip, the only security measure available at that time, making it difficult for the "good Samaritan" who stopped within minutes to free them. Finally the windshield was broken, and Sondra's little body was pulled from beneath her mother's.

There was nothing that could be done for Babe. In the last seconds before impact, Babe had thrown her body across the one most precious to her, her daughter. She had to know the risk she was taking. She had to know the danger she was in. She had to know it would be her life instead of her daughter's. But she did it anyway.

The kind man who stopped to help prayed for forty-five minutes into the ear of a nine-year-old who was confused and broken and bleeding and crying—but who was still alive.

Yes, Babe died for only one person, but isn't that enough? A mother's love was never greater illustrated than in a car one October morning in 1952.

You may get your
looks from your mother,
but you get your eternity
from your Father, your
heavenly Father.

max lucado

chapter two

A daughter's destiny

My Daughter of *Destiny,*

Even before you were born,
I *ordained* each and
every day of your life.

I know the plans I have just for you.
Watch Me *faithfully* complete
the *good* work I've started in you.

Tenderly,
Your Heavenly Father

—from Psalm 139:16; Jeremiah 29:11; Philippians 1:6

What will you do today? Not sure yet? Without much thought at all, you will probably wake up and continue what you started the day before. You might fold the clothes you left in the dryer. You might make up the bed you slept in. You might read another chapter in the novel you're reading. If you're a student, you might turn in homework you worked on last night. Whatever you do, chances are it will involve continuing what was already begun.

As a daughter, you are a continuation of what was started long before you were born. That's just the way life is: It is passed from one generation to the next. Life is a series of connecting events—a continuation, another chapter, a sequel, if you will. However you want to say it, life goes on.

Daughter, what is your destiny? How will you fit into the continuing cycle of life? No one knows the whole answer to that question. You will probably accomplish more than your parents ever dreamed possible. While your destiny may not include carrying on the family line physically, part of your destiny is simply to carry out many of the traditions and activities started by your parents and grandparents. What an awesome blessing!

You might remember the end of the Porky Pig cartoon—"That's all, folks!" Well, daughter, your birth assured your parents and grandparents that it's not over yet—you are here to carry on what they and their parents before them began. So stay tuned, and see you next week!

You have within you now
all the elements that are
necessary to make you all
the Father dreamed that you
would be in *Christ*.

e.w.
kenyon

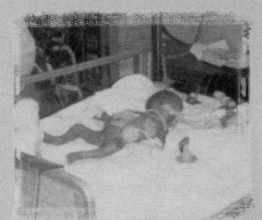

As gently as he could, the
doctor informed Jeff and Alicyn
that Amy would require surgery
to repair a heart valve that was
smaller than a cat hair.

with this ring

*S*he came too early, willing her way into a world she knew nothing about. How could she know she may be too small to survive? How could she know it would take weeks before her parents wouldn't cry anymore and before her grandparents wouldn't grieve for both their children and their first grandchild? She couldn't know. She only knew it was her time to be born.

Jeff and Alicyn had married young, against everyone's better judgment except their own. But Alicyn was pregnant, and they did love each other. They stressed to both sets of parents that they weren't getting married because they "had to"; they were getting married because they loved each other. It didn't take long for the newlyweds to discover that life had many lessons to teach them. Their love was soon tested.

The pregnancy had been uneventful. Alicyn was young and felt healthy, with the exception of the first two months when every smell she encountered was offensive. The young couple had rededicated their lives to God, and their families had joined them in their excitement about a new baby.

But no one was excited when Alicyn went into labor at twenty-eight weeks and when baby Amy was born weighing just one pound, fifteen ounces—or nine hundred grams, as it was officially recorded. Little Amy lay in her incubator with so many tubes and wires surrounding her that she looked like a tiny switchboard operator.

Several times a day, Jeff and Alicyn made the journey to the hospital to stand beside Amy for the fifteen-minute visits the Intensive Care Unit allowed: 8:00–8:15, 12:00–12:15, 3:00–3:15, and so it went. For three months, Amy maintained an unsteady balance between life and death. Jeff and Alicyn learned the true meaning of sacrificial love: giving their time, their energy, and their money.

As Amy neared the one-month mark, her tiny body got tinier as her weight dropped to one pound, twelve ounces. The doctor told the young couple that he suspected a heart murmur, which was common in premature babies. As gently as he could, the doctor informed Jeff and Alicyn that Amy would require surgery to repair a heart valve that was smaller than a cat hair. Jeff and Alicyn were devastated to realize what Amy would have to go through, but days earlier they had turned Amy over to God. Their prayers had been that God would keep Amy free of pain and give them the strength to handle whatever happened. They both knew that their most important job in life would be to get Amy to heaven, and if she were to die now, their mission would be completed.

Jeff was so fascinated by her small size that one evening, while Amy was still in the hospital, he had placed one of Alicyn's rings on her arm—and it went all the way up to her shoulder. It was one of those really big life-moments for Jeff. Seeing that ring on Amy's arm made the reality of their terrifying adventure grab his heart like a vice. His heart ached as his thoughts turned to every occasion he could envision his daughter receiving a ring—a birthday, graduation, engagement, and then marriage. Would she make it to all those events? Tears streamed down Jeff's cheeks, and once again he prayed for his daughter.

Little Amy persevered. Weighing a mere four pounds, eleven ounces at the age of three months and with a scar halfway around her body, she was finally able to move into her red-and-white–gingham Raggedy Ann bedroom. But life's lessons were not quite over for Jeff and Alicyn, as Amy had to be fed every three hours. There would be no more evenings of uninterrupted TV and no more weekends of sleeping in. Someone smaller than a newspaper had changed all that.

Their evenings were spent pacing the floor, rocking and singing, all the while praying for complete healing. They set an alarm clock to go off several times each night so they could make sure that Amy was breathing. Amy's reflexes were underdeveloped, and she sometimes couldn't breathe or swallow sufficiently. And the doctor had warned them that only time would tell whether Amy had suffered any brain damage. Yet they were amazed at how much they loved Amy and even more amazed that they were capable of caring for someone so small and fragile.

The days and weeks and months and, finally, the years passed—and Amy grew. Her little scar faded into her body, though it remained visible to remind her of her brush with death. More important, it reminded her of the healing power of God. Amy rode bikes, played basketball, ran up and down the street, and enjoyed her role as big sister.

As time passed, Jeff never forgot the feeling he had that night when he placed Alicyn's ring on Amy's arm. Amy's sixteenth birthday was coming up soon, and he wanted to do something special to honor the life of his firstborn. She had truly been a survivor, and he was very proud of her. So he planned a night of blessings for her. He invited her closest friends and family to be a part, asking them each to say something about Amy to encourage her as she grew into adulthood. He had a video made of her life, chronicling her difficult beginning and ending with the beautiful smile of a happy sixteen-year-old. Amy felt very special and very loved.

At the end of the evening, with tears in his eyes, Jeff told the story of the ring and how his dreams for his daughter's life had been challenged. He told of Alicyn and her devotion to Amy and how she, more than he, had endured sleepless nights to care for Amy. He then took the ring from Alicyn's finger and presented it to Amy. As he did, he said these words: "There is no greater love than the love a parent has for a child. Amy, you have taught us so much about life and love and God's richest blessings. With this ring, we rededicate our lives to you. As you enter into adulthood, know that we will stand beside you through every adventure, great and small. This ring stands as a symbol of your physical growth and as a reminder of our devotion to you. This ring connects you to us in a way many parents never experience. We were not sure the ring would ever fit your precious finger. So your mother and I now give you this ring."

And the ring that once went to Amy's shoulder now fit perfectly on her finger. Dad, mom, daughter, and a roomful of loving friends cried tears of joy for a gift they had been given sixteen years earlier and allowed to keep.

We must dream,
because we are made in
the image of Him who
sees things that are not
and wills them to be.

gary
hardaway

chapter three

A daughter's differences

My One-of-a-Kind
Daughter,

I've made you *wonderfully*

and divinely unique,

equipping you with special *gifts*

to serve Me and others as only you can.

differences

Y ou are My *masterpiece,*
created in Jesus Christ
to do the good works I've prepared
in advance especially for *you.*

B ecause of My extravagant *grace,*
you'll always have all the resources
you need to excel in making a *difference.*

Purposefully,
Your Creator

—from Psalm 139:14; 1 Corinthians 7:7; Ephesians 2:10; 2 Corinthians 9:8

Have you ever known a family who looked just alike? It's fascinating, isn't it? Two or three kids with the same hair color, the same color eyes, the same smile. Even the mom and dad, though not blood related, may look alike.

Scientists continue to study genetics and chromosomes in an effort to understand human development better. Cloning, a popular topic right now, is being touted as the next step in genetic engineering. The world is fascinated with the possibility of creating something exactly like something else. God's natural cloning is in the form of twins or triplets. Who isn't stopped in their tracks when a set of identical twins walks by? Who doesn't turn up the television when a story about septuplets comes on?

By all appearances, God has created multiple people who

look just alike. But study after study shows that appearances can be deceiving and that same-color hair and eyes don't necessarily make for the same personality.

You may look just like your mother, but you are not your mother. You may have some of the same physical features and many of the same personality traits as your dad, but you are uniquely your own person. Like each snowflake, God created each of us to be different. You have your own likes and dislikes, your own dreams and goals. David praises God in Psalm 139 for fearfully and wonderfully making him. God did that for you also. He "wove" you together as He did David and billions of others. Yes, you are very much like your parents— rejoice in your inheritance. But also rejoice in your differences —God does!

There has never been a package like you ever before in history, nor will there ever be *again*.

laurie beth jones

Even without their backpacks, the climb was difficult. The snow was so deep they didn't dare step out of line, and the wind blew so fiercely that Karen was afraid Annie would blow right off the mountain.

the adventure

*H*ow can you fight over Cheerios?" Dennis asked, being careful not to let the tone of his voice show how trivial he thought the fight had been. But Karen knew the fight wasn't just about Cheerios. It was about everything.

"She's only three," Dennis carefully continued. Then he waited for his wife to vent some more of her anger over the behavior of their much-loved and much-wanted daughter, Annie.

"Okay, you stay home with her tomorrow, if you think it's so easy," Karen said under her breath as she stormed out of the room.

That conversation had taken place twelve years earlier after Annie and Karen had disagreed about who was responsible for picking up the Cheerios that Annie had deliberately poured out on the kitchen floor. The next twelve years had been spent in many similar disagreements. Annie was never really comfortable with anyone else being in charge, and Karen was never comfortable with a child who wanted to be the boss. Consequently, Karen spent many hours reading parenting books and listening to advice from well-meaning friends. But, to put it mildly, Annie was difficult. The words *strong-willed* and *stubborn* were frequently used in the same sentence as Annie's name.

As the years passed, Annie did learn to mind her parents. In her own way, she respected them and loved them. She just wasn't sure they were always right. She questioned most every decision concerning her welfare. Karen and Dennis learned early on to pick their battles and to let Annie make a few mistakes along the way. Most important, they learned to pray for their relationship with Annie and for Annie's spiritual growth. It hadn't been easy, but they felt they were on the right track when Annie came home with Paul.

Paul was nice enough to them, but Karen had heard

through friends at church that he was not the best influence for a fifteen-year-old. He was seventeen and not a Christian, and his grades were less than what Karen and Dennis had expected out of Annie. They could see past the baggy jeans and spiky hair if he just didn't have that eyebrow ring!

"What does she see in him?" Karen begged for a reasonable answer to her question, but Dennis couldn't give her one—at least not one she was happy with.

"Maybe she just needs some attention. Let's take her away for the weekend," Dennis suggested.

"Now where could we go that would make Annie happy to be away with just her parents?" Karen asked with her eyes rolling and her head shaking. Sometimes Dennis forgot that his daughter wasn't three anymore and that problems weren't solved by a trip to the zoo.

"You're right," Dennis sighed. "We just have to stick to our guns about dating. She can only see him here at the house or at church events where there is a crowd. Who knows, maybe we can help him."

"Right now, I'm just interested in helping our daughter!" Karen wanted to scream.

It was February when Annie had first introduced them

to Paul, and the months that followed had been pretty rough. It seemed as if a major discussion erupted every night. "Where are you going? Who will be there? Is Paul going to be there? Have you done your homework?" Karen didn't know how much more she could take, but she knew she loved Annie and was determined to get her raised to adulthood.

Please, God, You know my limitations! You know I need Your guidance as the ultimate parent who has raised many difficult children. Put something in our lives to help Annie see that we love her and are only trying to help her.

As the end of the school year approached, Karen anticipated the summer months and Annie's having more free time. She began searching for activities to fill Annie's days. *Should I help her get a job? Should I make her go to church camp? Should I just handcuff her to me for three months?* The latter sounded the least appealing but perhaps the safest.

The phone rang as Karen was preparing for bed. Annie had just left her room asking permission to have Paul come over Friday night. The two months Annie and Paul had been dating had not improved Karen's first impression of him. He mumbled when he talked and showed absolutely no sign of ambition. But still, Annie had asked politely, so Karen agreed to let them watch movies at their house.

"Hello," Karen said into the receiver.

"Mrs. Kimball?" said the young man on the other end.

"Yes," Karen replied. "How can I help you?"

"Mrs. Kimball, this is Josh Miller, the new youth minister at your church."

"Why, of course, Josh, I've been meaning to meet you, but I guess our paths just haven't crossed yet. You can just call me Karen. You don't have to be so formal."

Karen wasn't quite ready to be Mrs. Kimball to people over twenty-five, and she was sure this young man was at least that old.

"Thanks, Karen," Josh said rather sheepishly. "I've been meaning to get to know you as well. I've enjoyed having Annie and Paul at our church activities."

"Well, thank you," Karen answered, bracing herself for the worst. She couldn't help but wonder if he was just buttering her up before he let her have it about her daughter and that boyfriend of hers.

"Karen, I need a chaperone for a youth trip this summer. I want to get parents more involved in youth activities, and

I would like you to go on a hiking adventure with us. You don't have to answer right now. You can tell me at church on Sunday."

"Josh," said Karen, "have Annie and Paul signed up for this trip?"

"Yes, I'm happy to say they have," answered Josh.

"Then I don't need to think about it. Sign me up," Karen said, not believing she had agreed to something she knew nothing about. But she did know that she was not going to let her child go with that boyfriend unless she went with them.

The end of the school year raced by, and soon it was time for the trip. The bus ride was uneventful—lots of singing and loud music but nothing too unnerving. Karen was surprised to see Annie and Paul interact with the other teenagers. For some reason she had envisioned them huddled under a blanket on the backseat with her fuming about their behavior the whole bus ride.

After two days on the bus, the group finally stood facing their demon. This was not going to be a hike in the park. The mountain was fourteen thousand feet of rock, snow, and wind gusts up to sixty miles an hour. Their backpacks weighed forty pounds apiece. Karen had spent six weeks in serious training, but she wasn't quite ready for this.

The first day went rather smoothly. Karen was exhausted but had enjoyed the work involved in the climb. Annie had not wanted to bunk in her mother's tent, so Karen quickly got to know the girls in her crew as they prepared supper for the evening. Then the youth minister gathered everyone up for a devotional.

"Get a rock," he told the group. "Look for one that is special to you but not too big."

Everyone went on a rock search then returned to the campfire.

Josh continued, "I want this rock to represent some barrier in your life. Something that keeps you from being the best you can be. I want you to struggle with that thing, whatever it is, this whole week. Every difficult breath you take, every step of your climb, I want you to push that barrier farther and farther behind you. Then when we reach the top of the mountain, I want you to leave it there. Just let it go and walk away."

This was not something Karen had anticipated about this trip. Sore muscles, tired feet, dizzying headaches, yes, she expected all that; but no one warned her that work on her inner self would be involved.

That night she prayed, "Dear God, open my eyes and my heart to what I need to know. Is this it? Is this the event to bring me closer to Annie? Please let this be it!"

The next day became more difficult. Annie suffered from altitude sickness and began throwing up. She worked her way up to her mother. Karen asked if she wanted to go back. "No," said Annie, "I can do it. I want to do it." But she didn't leave Karen's side the rest of the day. Paul was there too. He offered to carry Annie's backpack to lighten her load. Karen helped Paul get it off her daughter's shoulders and tied it around the already heavy weight he had on his back.

Paul talked gently to Annie, reassuring her that she could do it and that he was going to help her.

That night Annie asked if she could sleep in Karen's tent. Karen was so excited she told Annie to sleep with her in her sleeping bag. Both mother and daughter were exhausted, but they spent hours talking about life. They giggled like two girls at a slumber party. Karen whispered stories of her own teenage years, and Annie revealed some concerns she also had about Paul. For the first time in many years—in a sleeping bag on the side of a mountain—Karen slept peacefully.

The next day was full of surprises. Annie was still weak, and Paul once again carried her backpack, but on this day, Karen talked to Paul. And she listened to him. Really listened. He wasn't so bad. He told her how important getting to come to church had been to him and how he wanted to learn more once he got home. He said he hoped Josh would study the Bible with him as soon as they got back.

By lunchtime they had reached high camp. Two more hours and they would reach the top. Backpacks were not necessary for the last leg of the trip. Everyone gladly took them off. Even without their backpacks, the climb was difficult. The snow was so deep they didn't dare step out of line, and the wind blew so fiercely that Karen was afraid Annie would blow right off the mountain. Paul reached the top first and extended a hand to Karen. He gripped her hand tightly and pulled her to the top. Together they reached for Annie, and soon the three of them were laughing, hugging, and crying.

"Annie, you made it!" Karen yelled to her daughter.

"Momma, we both made it. We made it together. Thank you for being there for me!"

"No problem" was Karen's sincere reply. With arms still wrapped around her daughter, Karen looked over Annie's shoulders to the splendor of snowcapped mountains and glorious sunshine. *Thank you, God, for the mountaintop experience of a lifetime.*

That night, around the campfire, many burdens were lifted. Karen and Annie had left their rocks at the top of the mountain and knew that they were ready to start over. Together they rejoiced in their differences and gave up the burden of resisting each other's love.

God loves you

and made you for

the pleasure of

knowing you.

sheila walsh

chapter four

A daughter's *debt*

My *Darling* Daughter,

Y̲ou're *unforgettable.*

In fact, I've engraved you

on the very palms of My hands.

I clothe you in garments of salvation.

You wear a robe of *righteousness.*

Because of My great love for you,

I made you *alive* in Christ.

You are My jewel.

I'll remember My *covenant*

with you forever.

Eternally,
Your Heavenly Father

—from Isaiah 49:16; 61:10; Ephesians 2:4–5; Psalm 111:5

It's a terrible feeling to "owe" someone something, isn't it? You go to the movie and discover that you don't have enough money for a coke, so you have to borrow. You say those dreaded words, "I'll pay you back." Is it harder on the one making the promise or the one receiving it? That's probably a tossup.

The one making the promise tries to mentally record the debt, knowing it may be forgotten before the movie starts; and the one making the loan knows it may be forgotten but doesn't want to make the friend feel awkward. But owing a debt is always an uncomfortable circumstance—

except when the lender forgives the debt entirely.

What a freeing experience to hear the words "Don't worry about it! I've got you covered." Translated, that means you don't have to repay the money and you don't have to feel guilty about it. Could you ever repay the hours, the money, the energy your parents spent on you? No way! Just like you could never repay Jesus for paying your debt at Calvary. There are times when a simple thank-you is enough. Today may be one of those times. Call your parents and say, "Thanks for all you've done for me." They've already forgiven your debt, you're just thanking them for doing so.

God made each of us unique, and there is a vast mystery and beauty surrounding the human *soul*.

alan loy mcginnis

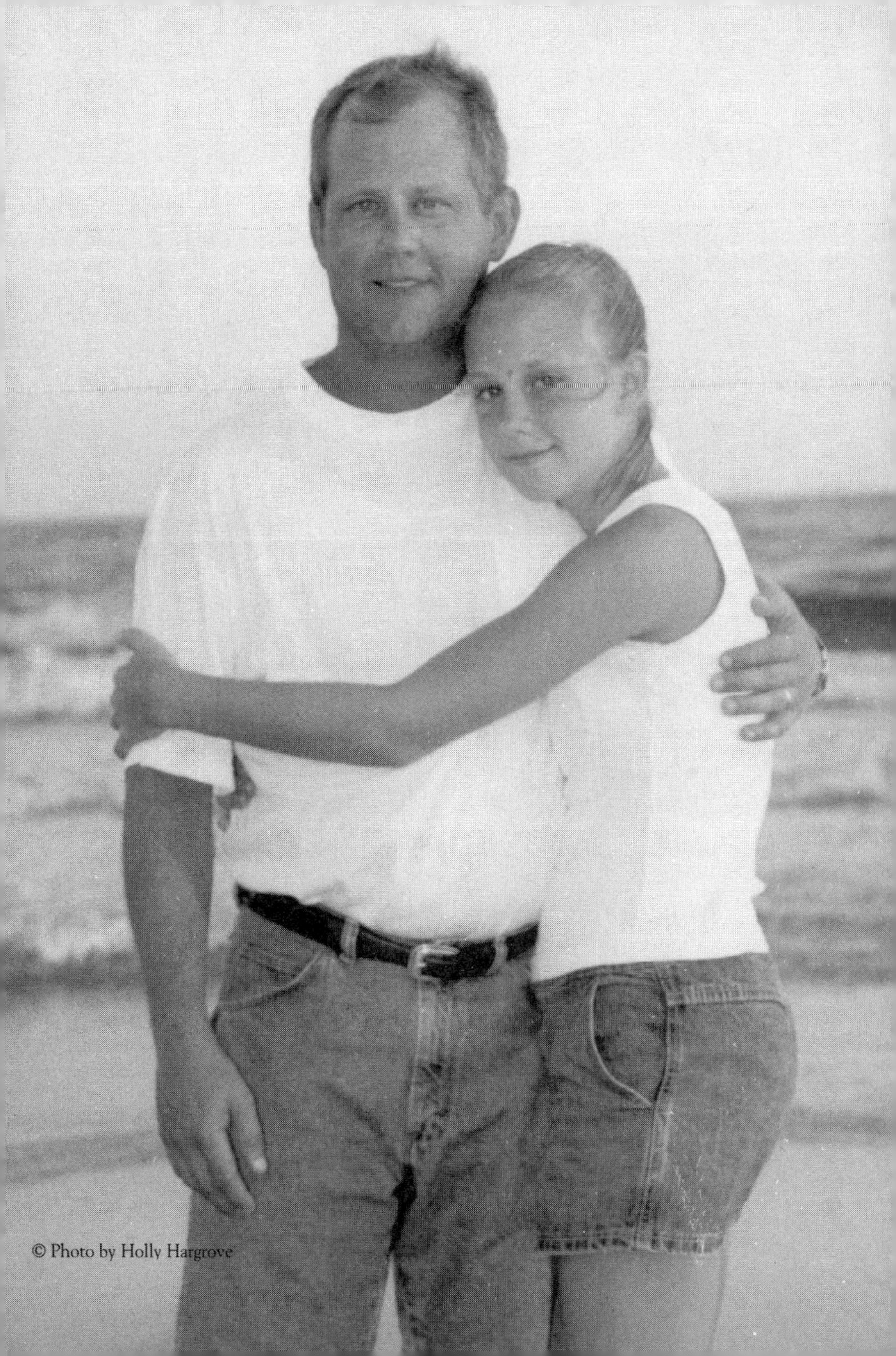

Amanda took a deep breath as the
music filled the auditorium. "I'm ready,
Daddy," she said as she picked up her
bouquet that had been decorating the
little rocking chair in the cry room for
the last thirty minutes.

going to the chapel

Amanda was a PK. That stands for "Preacher's Kid," and sometimes she wasn't very happy about the title. But, today, she was thrilled. At twenty-three, she was very proud of her preacher daddy and, most important, very excited that he was going to perform her wedding ceremony.

Everything appeared to be ready. Amanda peeked through the glass window from the cry room out into the church auditorium. It was breathtakingly beautiful. Lining the pews were yards and yards of ribbon, white bows made of satin, and bouquets of daisies. An archway, covered in greenery and more daisies, awaited the couple at the front of the room. And the final touch—the touch Amanda had always dreamed of—hundreds of softly lit candles gave a romantic glow to what was usually a very normal, small, plain church auditorium.

Amanda's mother had worked hard to make this day special for her. One of Amanda's friends had warned her that planning the wedding would be a disaster. She said that Amanda and her mom would disagree on everything and that by the time the wedding day arrived, Amanda would wish she had eloped. But it hadn't been true. From the first color picked to the last shower given, Amanda and her mother had just had fun. Along with Amanda's joy for the day, she felt a little sad that it would soon be over. She realized that the fun she and her mother had shared was unique, and she wasn't quite ready for it to end.

"No, no tears. I'm not going to cry," Amanda said out loud to herself as she tried to brush away all sad thoughts.

Holding tightly to the faded, tan curtain that was intended to keep the congregation from witnessing small children at play, Amanda was careful not to let herself be seen as she peeked out from her hiding place. She spotted her dad giving something to her mom. *I wonder what that is,* she thought. *It looks like a Bible, but it's not the one he uses on Sundays. He has something up his sleeve that he hasn't told me about.*

Amanda's dad wasn't really what you would call "hard-headed," but you would call him a "stickler" when it came to rules. Amanda had learned at an early age that there was no bargaining with Dad, but at the same time, she never doubted his love for her and her brother, Scott. While it was true that, from time to time, they both found it to their advantage to go to their mother first, they respected him and his position in the church. Watching him move among the flowers and bows, Amanda thought of the many camping trips they used to take. She was always shocked at how easily he could put a worm on a hook but would cringe if he stood within two feet of anyone who was holding a sucker. He hated that sticky feeling, he would say. Or how he could live in a tent in the rain for a week but couldn't stand for one book to be out of place in his office. "That's my dad," Amanda said softly under her breath.

The clock in the room seemed to grow and jump right off the wall at her saying, "It's seven o'clock and time for your wedding!"

debt

The "wedding planner," her Aunt Jo, opened the door. "It's time," she said merrily.

"Just one minute," Amanda said.

Aunt Jo shut the door and Amanda prayed, "Dear God, be with me this day. Thank You for the gift of both my physical family and my church family who are here today to support Brian and me. Help me to always be the example You want me to be as a wife and, one day, as a mother. I pray that I can be everything my parents have been to me when I have a daughter of my own. Especially be with Daddy today. This will be hard for him. In Jesus name, amen."

Amanda heard a soft knock at the door, and then her daddy's hand gently pushed it open. "Ready, chickadee?" he asked. He had called her chickadee since she was two. She had cried for a baby chicken at Easter, but he had not wanted her to have one. Always the practical one, "It will just die," he had warned her. But he finally gave in, and the little yellow chicken refused to die. It was Amanda's first pet.

Amanda took a deep breath as the music filled the auditorium. "I'm ready, Daddy," she said as she picked up her bouquet that had been decorating the little rocking chair in the cry room for the last thirty minutes. She took one last look in the mirror, decided she needed more lip gloss, and then walked over to join her daddy for the walk she had dreamed of since she was a little girl.

Arm in arm they walked to the back of the auditorium. The crowd still had their eyes on the flower girl and ring bearer as they made their way to the front of the church and had not yet noticed that Amanda had taken her place. Amanda was glad they hadn't seen her yet. She wanted this one moment with just her dad, and she blocked out the crowd and looked over at him. He was nervous, she could tell, because he was rocking. He always rocked when he was nervous. Back and forth from his toes to his heels. *Funny,* she thought, *how he can preach every Sunday and still be nervous about this. I guess it's not the preaching part he's nervous about,* she concluded with a smile. She wanted to kiss him on the cheek and tell him she loved him, but she knew he would start crying, so she decided to wait.

Amanda's attention went back to the auditorium, where everyone was now standing. It was time to walk. Her daddy placed his hand over her arm and gently nudged her forward. *So this is what it feels like,* Amanda thought to herself.

I love it. There's Elizabeth and John Mark. Neat, Mrs. McKenna came. And Grandma and Grandpa. They look great! There's Mama. Don't cry, Mama. Remember, we talked about this. I'm doing good. Don't start crying. You look beautiful.

Amanda couldn't believe she was actually able to think. She was glad, though. She wanted to remember every detail. Her best friends looked beautiful. Yes, she had made the right choice in their dresses. And the groomsmen, they were so handsome. Pretty impressive wedding party, she had to admit.

Then her eyes met Brian's. She wasn't sure she had ever seen a smile so big. He looked as if his chest were going to pop open. She tried to send a telepathic message to her "almost" husband: *Breathe, Brian. I don't want you to faint.* It must have worked because she noticed his chest relax as he let out a soft sigh. Amanda thought how perfect he was for her.

It was over. The walk was over, and now they stood at the front of the church. Amanda's mother stood and handed a Bible to her daddy, and together they made a statement about giving their daughter to Brian. Then Amanda and

Brian turned around to face the room full of the friends and family who had come to share the day with them.

"Amanda," her daddy began, "I have to start with a little story. I have to admit that when I was a young preacher, my focus wasn't always where it should have been. I was sometimes more interested in appearances than in the truth. I had been given a beautiful Bible to preach out of and had proudly displayed it on my desk, intending to hold it up every Sunday for all to see. But then I had a little girl—a little girl whom I loved more than any possession. She taught me many things.

"One day she came into my office and opened my beautiful Bible and wrote all over the first page. I was devastated. I wondered how I would explain the incident to the person who had given that Bible to me as a gift. I remember picking up the Bible and looking down at that little girl, ready to scold her for her actions. But you, Amanda, looked up at me and sweetly said, 'I write *Amanda*.' That's when it dawned on me that I also wanted Amanda's name written in the Book of Life. So I took my pen and wrote, 'Amanda, age 2, December 15, 1975.' My goal has always been to do whatever I could to ensure that your name, Amanda, has stayed in the Book of Life. I'm giving this Bible to you today. Write your children's names in it, and do everything you possibly can to ensure that their names stay there."

Amanda took the Bible from her daddy and opened it to the first page. There she saw her scribbling and her daddy's explanation. There was no stopping the tears now, as Amanda realized—now more than ever—how much her daddy loved her.

We can consider ourselves a loved person, not because of our circumstances or situations but simply because God loves us perfectly, totally and eternally.

dreams

A daughter's dreams

Dreams

My Wonderful Daughter,

You're *royalty!* I've chosen you,
calling you out of darkness
into My marvelous light.

Diligently seek Me first
with all your *heart*
and then watch Me bless yo

Y ou'll discover that
My plans for you
far exceed your
most incredible
dreams.

R emember, all things
are possible because I'm your Father.
I've given you birth into *living hope!*

Majestically,
Your King of Kings

dreams

—from 1 Peter 2:9; Matthew 6:33; Ephesians 3:20; Mark 10:27; 1 Peter 1:3

When you close your eyes, what do you see? In the stillness of night, what do you dream? It's not really the dreams you have at night that you hope will come true; it's those you dream when you're totally awake.

For instance, what do you dream about when you're sitting alone on the porch or when you're faking attention in a history class? Those are the dreams that really matter. It's during those quiet times that you are planning your future and what you want it to look like. It's hard, isn't it? Sometimes the dreams you have for yourself and the dreams others have for you are not the same.

Parents, grandparents, teachers, coaches, youth ministers, husbands—it may seem that everyone has a little piece of you. You don't want to disappoint those who love you, yet you have to be true to yourself. Read Hebrews 12:2 for a fresh perspective: "Let us fix our eyes on Jesus, the author and perfecter of our faith, who for the joy set before him endured the cross, scorning its shame, and sat down at the right hand of the throne of God." Focusing on Jesus is essential! If you try to fulfill the dreams other people have for you—or even the dreams you have for yourself—instead of pursuing the dreams Jesus has for you, you will not find true fulfillment.

Those who keep their eyes fixed on Jesus can be assured that their dreams and goals will lead to an eternal victory. No, you cannot please everyone, and yes, there are many great mentors you may pattern your life after. But when you put Jesus first, you know you will be a winner!

How special to know that God dreams because each girl, through Him, has potential stretched and carved and carefully ordained for bright, happy, fulfilled *tomorrows*.

ann kiemel-anderson

She knew she wasn't supposed to
want things that belonged to other
people, but she couldn't help it.
Well, she finally told herself, if
I can't have it, then I'm glad
Mary Alice will get it!

mary alice's birthday party

On September 12, 1959, Melissa Ward's attitude on life took a major turn for the better. That day was Mary Alice Farmer's birthday party. Mary Alice was Melissa's very best friend in the whole world. She lived down the street and around the corner from Melissa. Down the street and around the corner wasn't too hard to get to in 1959. Kids were allowed to ride their bikes all over the neighborhood and even stay out until dark, without once reporting in.

As a matter of fact, mommas in 1959 insisted that children play outside. They weren't to be "underfoot," as Melissa's mother used to say when she and her brothers hung around the kitchen asking for something. Whenever Melissa would come inside, her mother would say, "What do you need?" implying that the only reason to come inside was because she needed something. Melissa guessed that was true because everything she *wanted* was outside, like friends and bikes and forts, while everything she *needed* was inside, like food and the bathroom.

That day, September 12, had already started out differently for Melissa. It was a Saturday, and her mother had asked her to stay in and help her wrap Mary Alice's birthday present. Melissa knew this was a grown-up job, and she was very flattered to be asked to help. "You can cut the paper and add any bow you want," her mother had said.

Melissa hadn't seen the present her mother had picked out for her to take. At seven years old, she was in school and missed out on most of her mother's shopping trips. But when she saw the present she instantly fell in love with it. It was a miniature mink stole with a matching mink muff. The fur was as white and fluffy as a baby rabbit. The back of the stole was covered in shiny white satin, the kind Melissa had seen on her aunt's wedding dress. A tiny hook and eye was discreetly sown into the front to close the stole, so that when it was worn, it looked like one piece of fabric. It was the most elegant thing Melissa had ever seen! *How glamorous I would look in that,* Melissa thought.

She knew she wasn't supposed to want things that belonged to other people, but she couldn't help it. *Well,* she finally told herself, *if I can't have it, then I'm glad Mary Alice will get it!*

Soon it was time to dress for the party. That, in itself, was an ordeal in 1959. Melissa's mother took out the best dress she had, laid it neatly on the ironing board, sprinkled it with water from a glass bottle that had a "sprinkler spout," and ironed and ironed as if she could make wrinkles go away and never return. Melissa knew those wrinkles would be back before she got to the party, but it was a mother's job to see that her daughter was clean and starched before a big event. And a birthday party was a big event.

Oh, the party itself wouldn't be elaborate by today's standards. Parties were always in the middle of the afternoon so mommas didn't have to feed their guests a meal. Skating and gymnastic parties didn't exist in 1959. It would just be at the honoree's house, and the children would play "Pin the Tail on the Donkey" or some other silly game. Everyone would sing "Happy Birthday" as the birthday girl blew out her candles. Then cake and ice cream would be served. Melissa wondered why she had to dress up at all. Her mother would tell her it wasn't respectful to attend a birthday party in play clothes, even though you were expected to play.

At a quarter of three, Melissa and her mother started the walk to Mary Alice's house. She had wanted to drive even though it was just down the street because they had a new station wagon with a backseat that faced the rear window. She thought she would look cool arriving in her new car and then jumping out from the backseat.

"It's a pretty day and the twins would enjoy the walk," her momma had said.

O great, thought Melissa, *not only do I have to walk, my brothers have to tag along.*

Melissa's brothers were three and quite a handful. Well, one was and one wasn't, but there were two of them; so even though one was quieter, together they were a handful.

"Come on, boys, Melissa will be late." Melissa's mother hurried the twins out the door.

Melissa's mother was right—the day was beautiful! Melissa loved the cool smell of fall in the air and the soft breeze making her hair lift off her shoulders. She even held hands with her brothers and challenged them to skip like she did.

At exactly three o'clock, they arrived at Mary Alice's door and rang the doorbell. The door opened and there stood Mary Alice in the most beautiful white, dotted-swiss party dress and a white, satin bow that pulled her hair just out of her eyes then positioned itself right on the side of her head.

"Come in," said Mary Alice. "I want you to meet my friends."

Her friends? How does she have friends I don't know? Where did they come from? Melissa felt a little betrayed at seeing the room full of people she had never met.

"These are friends from my Sunday school class," Mary Alice explained. Melissa had heard about Sunday school, but she had never been. Sundays were different, she knew that, but mostly because Daddy made pancakes and her family stayed home and watched their new TV. Melissa wasn't so sure about school on another day of the week.

Melissa had such fun at the party, and she truly enjoyed Mary Alice's friends. They were all so nice to her. Mary

Alice loved the mink stole. Another friend had given her play high heels, so she really did look glamorous with the shoes and the mink on.

As the party was winding down, Melissa mustered up her courage and asked, "Why do you go to Sunday school?"

"Well," said Mary Alice, "I go to meet new friends and to learn more about Jesus."

Melissa understood how much fun it would be to meet new friends, but she had one more question. "Who is Jesus?" she wanted to know.

With all the wisdom of a seven-year-old, Mary Alice simply said, "He made us and now He watches over us and loves us no matter what."

Melissa's mother came at precisely five o'clock to pick her up. She had left the twins with Melissa's daddy, so it would be just the two of them on the walk home. Melissa felt that today was her lucky day.

As the leaves fell and the temperature dropped, Melissa and her mother huddled together for a brisk walk home. Melissa's mother asked all the usual questions about the party—"How was the cake? Did Mary Alice like her presents? Who was there?" Then she asked the most unusual question. "If you could wish for anything in the whole world, what would you like to have?"

Melissa was truly stunned. She had never thought about what she would want if she could have *anything*—anything in the whole world. She couldn't believe that her mother was asking her that question. *Does this mean she would give me whatever I ask for?*

Melissa's mind was racing. She really liked that stole. She had nearly cried watching Mary Alice open it. It was so beautiful. But something else nagged at her seven-year-old soul, and she finally blurted it out: "Mom, I want us to go to church like Mary Alice does!"

After she'd said it, she couldn't believe she had done it. Her mother was quiet for what seemed like forever and then managed a "We'll see." But the very next Sunday, Melissa and her whole family sat on the pew next to Mary Alice and her whole family.

Who would have ever thought a birthday party, a special wish, and a seven-year-old girl could change the course of a family?

God did.

chapter six

A daughter's diary

My Precious Daughter,

I've lavished My *love* upon you,
calling you My child.
I know every thought you think
even before *you* think it.

diary

I even know the *secrets* you try to hide,

fearing rejection.

But don't worry, nothing in your past, present,

or *future* could ever stop Me from *loving* you.

Never forget that you are *forever* loved

and that I'm thinking good thoughts of you.

No matter where you go, I'm always with you.

My *faithfulness* continues through all generations.

Hugs,
God

—from 1 John 3:1; Psalm 139:1–18; Romans 8:38–39; Psalm 119:90

Webster's dictionary defines a diary as "a daily record," but any girl knows that a diary is so much more. A daily record is a plan book or a calendar or something—but it's not a *diary*.

A diary is full of delicious dreams and exciting encounters and captivating conversations not meant for all to hear. A diary has a tiny key that must be hidden from younger brothers and sisters. What was Webster thinking when he defined a diary as "a daily record"? He must not have had a diary of his own!

Do you know that whether or not you have written one word about your life, it has still been recorded?

Your mom and dad have carefully recorded each event from field trips to weddings in their minds. It's a little unsettling to think someone knows almost as much about you as you do. But it's also a little comforting.

It's nice to be known so well and loved for all of who you are—the good and the bad of you. But there will be things in your life that your parents will never know. There is only one other besides you who will know it all—God. As a matter of fact, He wrote in your diary before you were even born, and He regularly unlocks it with the tiny key He keeps close to His heart and continues to write out the chapters of your life.

God has seen your movie—
the whole story of your whole
life—and he loves *you*.

sheila
walsh

The jet she was now riding in

was her vehicle to realizing a

lifelong dream, and it was also

a confirmation that God still

moves mountains.

to russia with love

*J*anice looked out the airplane window and saw a great sea of brilliant, blue sky and fluffy, white clouds. Such a simple combination, yet filled with majesty and peace. *Where were airplanes in God's ultimate plan for humankind?* Janice wondered. *Did He craft them in the minds of our ancestors for travel or for confirmation of His greatness?*

Janice was happy with either answer. The jet she was now riding in was her vehicle to realizing a lifelong dream, and it was also a confirmation that God still moves mountains.

Janice looked over at her mother, Pat, who was just settling in with a good book. Her mother was an avid reader. When she wasn't reading a book, she was listening to one being read to her on a cassette. Consequently, Pat was a master at trivia. Janice had always joked with her mother that she would make a good contestant on the game show *Jeopardy*.

"Pat Robinson, Rostov-on-Don," Janice said to her mother, mimicking a game-show host.

Pat smiled and answered, "What's the name of the city in Russia where the most beautiful little girl waits for her mother?"

"Good answer," said Janice.

It was the best answer. Janice was on her way to pick up her soon-to-be adopted baby girl, and she couldn't quit smiling. Janice had always believed this day would come. What she hadn't known was that it would involve a trip halfway around the world.

Janice's trouble began when she was just fourteen. She had had cramps so severe she would miss school for three days each month. Her doctor finally advised her parents that a hysterectomy would be the only solution. Pat and her husband had been towers of strength for their daughter, but they couldn't help feeling a loss for the grandchildren they would never have.

As the years passed, Janice tried not to dwell on her plight. She enjoyed her high school years just like her friends did; fashion trends and boyfriends were the main topic of slumber-party discussions. It was only late at night with her mother that Janice would talk about her fear of telling the man she would marry that she wouldn't be able to have his children. Pat would wrap her arms around her daughter and remind her of the story of Abraham and Isaac when Isaac questioned his father about the sacrificial lamb.

"The wood and the fire are here, but where is the lamb?" Isaac had asked.

"God will provide," Abraham had reassured his son.

"God will provide for you too," Pat would tell her daughter. Janice knew the end of the story of Abraham and Isaac. She had read that story many times, but her story was not written down anywhere. While she trusted God, her teenage years were still spent wondering how that chapter of her life would be written.

Janice's mom had been right. Janice had married a

wonderful man three years earlier. They began dating during Janice's sophomore year of college, and he had proposed during her junior year. Randy came from a big family, and Janice had dreaded the night she had to tell him what their future would hold.

"We'll adopt," he had quickly responded.

Janice knew then that he was the one she wanted to spend the rest of her life with. Their beautiful wedding was held the summer after she graduated from college.

On their first anniversary, Janice knew it was time to start looking for a good adoption agency. Randy agreed and suggested that she start with the Internet. It seemed too easy. They both thanked God that they lived during this time of easy access to the whole world. It soon became apparent that an international adoption would be the fastest, so they settled on an agency in New Jersey.

Things moved very quickly, and the next thing they knew, Randy and Janice were headed to Moscow. From Moscow they flew to Rostov-on-Don, where they would eventually meet their daughter.

"Do you think she'll have blond hair?" Randy had whispered, after being greeted by a blond stewardess, a blond taxi driver, and now a blond orphanage director.

"I don't care what color her hair is," Janice whispered back. "I just want to take her home!"

They both smiled at the director as they were led into orphanage number three. They had been told that it was one of the better orphanages. Janice had braced herself for the worst but was surprised at how neat and orderly the room was. There were fifteen baby beds lined up against the wall. The women looking after the babies were very protective of them, and the babies seemed happy and well fed.

They were then led into the director's office, where a translator was waiting to help them with the negotiations. Almost immediately, a woman appeared with a blond-haired, blue-eyed little girl.

"She will fit in very well with your family," the translator told Janice and Randy.

Randy and Janice just stared at her, afraid to move. Afraid if they did, she might disappear.

"You can hold her," the translator said.

Janice reached out and gently pulled her close. This was

her baby. She knew it. Although the baby wouldn't make eye contact with Janice, she didn't cry, and Janice felt an instant bond with her.

The Russian woman motioned that she had to take the baby back. Janice reluctantly gave her to the woman, but not before she kissed her and told her she would see her soon. The translator went on to tell them that they would have to stay a week to work on the adoption papers. They would be allowed to see the little girl only one hour the whole week. Janice and Randy looked at each other in disbelief, but they knew they were on foreign ground and had to play by someone else's rules.

Paperwork and sightseeing filled their week, and as the time for their return flight neared, they called home to tell their family when they would arrive. But the day before their departure, they were told they would have to come back later for their daughter. The paperwork would take another two months. With tears in their eyes, they boarded the plane for home. Although their daughter wasn't in their arms, she was certainly in their hearts. They knew they would be back.

Now Janice was on her way once again to Russia. Randy

couldn't take any more time off from his job, so Janice had asked Pat to go. Pat, a mother who had stood by her daughter as her dream to have a baby was taken away, would now stand beside her as her dream was revived.

Pat had been right—God would provide.

chapter seven

A daughter's *devotion*

My Beloved Daughter,

Trouble and heartache
are *guaranteed* components
of life on earth.

devotion

But be *assured,*

I'll never leave you

or abandon you—

no matter what you're facing.

I, Myself, go before you

and am with you.

I am your *helper;*

you can trust Me

to faithfully meet all your needs

according to My *unlimited* riches in *glory.*

Devotedly,
Your Excellent God

devotion

—from John 16:33; Hebrews 13:5–6; Deuteronomy 31:8; Philippians 4:19

What's your job as a daughter? What are your responsibilities? Do you do the dishes after supper? Are you in charge of the laundry? Is cleaning the bathroom one of your chores? Somewhere around the time you were five or six, you were probably given a job or two to help around the house. And with every dish you loaded into the dishwasher and every towel you folded, you learned what it meant to help out.

Those memories may not be your favorite. Still, you know your parents sacrificed for you and that you need to give back to them. You are as devoted to them as they are to you.

As you age, your jobs will change. You will no longer wash their dishes, for you will have your own to do. You won't do their laundry;

you'll do your own. But your devotion and love for them will cause you to drop by on the weekend and check in. You'll have them over for dinner or drive your mom to the beauty shop. You might paint their house or plant a bed of pansies.

Then one day you'll care for them as they cared for you. One of your parents may someday need all the care of a newborn. And you will be there to do whatever is needed. You'll do it because you are a devoted daughter and the child of a loving God, who has never left you and never will.

What a great example Jesus is of a child whose obedient heart led Him to leave His home and His Father and come to set us free! If He could do that for His Father, what can you do for yours?

Only God knew what was best for me, where I would fit into the world. And I trusted him to bring my dreams into line with his dreams for *me*.

heather whitestone

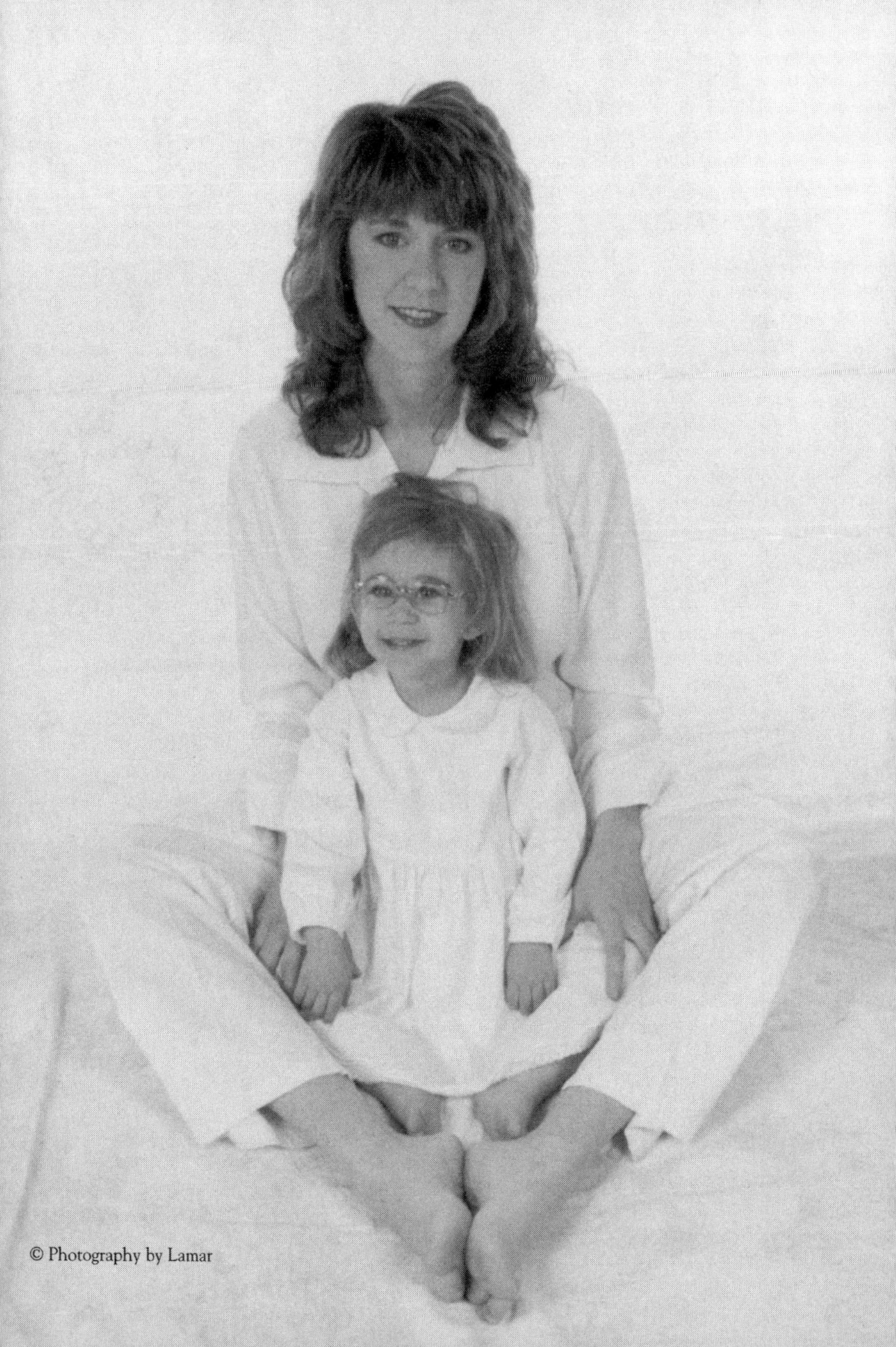

The mother-daughter part of

their relationship had been

secured years ago, but their

teatime had sealed

their friendship.

tea, anyone?

How do you prepare to be an orphan? I wonder if there's a book about living without your parents. If there is, I don't suppose it would be geared to middle-aged adults! Marsha pondered these thoughts as she gently fluffed her mother's pillows and straightened the top of the nightstand that held the barrage of medications her mother needed to get through each day. *Okay, maybe I'm the one to write that book. Let's see...here's a title—Left Behind. Oh, that's already been used, you say. Okay, I'll keep thinking. Maybe I need to stop thinking! I'm beginning to answer myself!* Marsha was truly concerned and, on some days, consumed with the thought of exactly that—being left behind.

Her father had passed away ten years earlier from a sudden heart attack. Marsha had been devastated. But time had helped heal her heart, and her own family had kept her so busy that she coped better than she had expected. But in ten years things had changed. Her children were grown now. Two of them were married with children; the third was content to live five hours away in the city. Her four grandchildren, a constant source of joy, were now all in school and required less of her time and attention.

Her husband, Robert, was still very involved in his real estate business. In the last ten years his company had grown so quickly that he was forced to spend more time at the office. Marsha didn't resent this at all. In fact, she knew he was working hard to prepare for their future together, when what he really wanted was to slow down. Maybe ten more years, he had told her just last weekend as they snuggled together on Saturday morning.

Marsha had analyzed life many times over the years and had concluded that everyone probably lived in ten-year cycles. Ten years is enough time to change just about anything: It could change a new house to a house needing repairs. Ten years could turn a bad marriage into a great one or a great marriage into a terrible one. Ten years is enough time to shape a child's future or the future of an entire country. Going from forty-five to fifty-five had certainly changed Marsha's life.

For the last year she had tenderly cared for her mother who had been diagnosed with cancer eighteen months earlier. Initially, the doctors had held out hope, but now—even after chemotherapy and radiation—tests showed that the cancer was not retreating.

At first Marsha just denied the whole thing. The doctors were wrong. The tests were wrong. They were all wrong. Mom would be fine. Marsha tried her best to keep everything the same. She insisted that her mom stay in her own little house, where she had friends and a garden, and Marsha went there to care for her every day. But eventually, reality sat in, and Marsha saw with her own eyes what the test tried to tell her. Her mom was not fine. She was very sick, and life would never be the same.

Once Marsha had accepted the truth of the cancer, she was surprised to find herself feeling angry. It was difficult to understand why the medical profession couldn't solve the problem. In some ways, she even faulted her mother. But only because her mother had always solved every other problem she had encountered. Moms are supposed to be able to make things right—but she couldn't make this one right, and Marsha was a little miffed about it. Of course that emotion didn't last long, and Marsha shifted wholeheartedly into the role of caregiver. Marsha asked her mother to move into their guest bedroom, and she did. The doctors had said her mother would live only about six more months, but she'd been with them a year now.

Being blessed with this extra time is a victory, isn't it? Marsha raised that question to no one in particular. An extra year, yes, it was a victory.

But why doesn't it feel like a victory?

"Marsha?" Betty called.

"Yes, Mom, I'm right here. What do you need?"

"Marsha, when you have time, I'd like to have some warm tea."

"Coming right up," Marsha said, trying to imitate a waitress at a Waffle House.

It was a morning ritual they had enjoyed for the past ten years. After Marsha had retired from teaching school, she found that she was so accustomed to leaving the house each morning that she just decided to go to her mother's house for tea three mornings a week. Of course there were weeks when Marsha couldn't fit three mornings into her schedule, and there were mornings where fifteen minutes would have to do when an hour was preferred. The great thing about it was that Marsha never felt "duty bound" to visit her mom. She went because it was a pleasure to see her friend, her mother.

Those words seem so odd together, Marsha thought. My mother, my friend. Marsha remembered a scene from her teenage years when she argued with her mother because she wouldn't let her go to a party. Marsha had pleaded with her to relax a little and let her go to more parties. Betty had told her that her first job was to be her mother. She said she had her feet in two boxes. One box had "Mother" on it, and the other had "Friend." Betty had explained, "I prefer to keep my feet in both boxes, but occasionally, I need to put both feet in the Mother box. I can assure you, however, that until you are grown, both of my feet will never be put in the Friend box."

Marsha shook her head as she remembered her mother's words and then remembered how she had also used them with her own children.

As Marsha poured the water into the pot, she realized how much the past ten years had meant to her. The mother-daughter part of their relationship had been secured years ago, but their teatime had sealed their friendship. Marsha's mind drifted to the many conversations about recipes and hairdos. She couldn't help but ask herself who in the world she could brag endlessly to about her own grandchildren when her mom was gone. And certainly she knew that there would be no one who would understand when she complimented or complained about her brother!

Only a mother understands some of the things a daughter feels. There is no replacement, Marsha concluded as she finished up the tea and poured it into one of the white china cups with blue periwinkles framing the top edge. Robert had joined the teatime in his own way by delighting Marsha with a collection of teacups for most any occasion he could think of. Marsha had joked with him that he was more in touch with his feminine side than he cared to admit. He would just raise his man-sized coffee cup and say, "Thank you," in a deeper-than-normal voice.

"All ready," Marsha said as she entered her mother's room. She opened the curtains to reveal a glorious day. The sun was shining, and the warm air of April in Louisiana had already taken the chill out of the bedroom.

"Mom, maybe we can sit outside this afternoon. That is, if you feel like it," Marsha commented.

"I'd like that," her mother answered.

Marsha knew that by this afternoon Betty would not feel like it, but it was okay to dream a little. Pulling a chair close to her mother's bed, Marsha settled in for a few more precious moments with the woman who had loved her more than any other woman ever would.

She kissed her on the cheek and said, "Thanks, Mom, for never stepping out of those boxes."

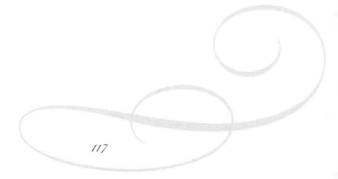

Look for these other *Hugs* books

Hugs for Teens
Hugs for Dad
Hugs for Friends
Hugs for Grads
Hugs for Grandma
Hugs for Grandparents
Hugs for Kids
Hugs for Mom
Hugs for Sisters
Hugs for Teachers
Hugs for the Holidays
Hugs for the Hurting
Hugs for Those in Love
Hugs for Women
Hugs to Encourage and Inspire
Hugs from Heaven: Celebrating Friendship
Hugs from Heaven: Embraced by the Savior
Hugs from Heaven: On Angel Wings
Hugs from Heaven: Portraits of a Woman's Faith
Hugs from Heaven: The Christmas Story